CATS

SCOTTISH FOLD CATS

by Elizabeth Andrews

Cody Koala

An Imprint of Pop!
popbooksonline.com

Hello! My name is Cody Koala

This book is filled with videos, puzzles, games, and more! Scan the QR codes* while you read, or visit the website below to make this book pop.

popbooksonline.com/scottish-fold

*Scanning QR codes requires a web-enabled smart device with a QR code reader app and a camera.

abdobooks.com

Published by Pop!, a division of ABDO, PO Box 398166, Minneapolis, Minnesota 55439. Copyright ©2023 by Abdo Consulting Group, Inc. International copyrights reserved in all countries. No part of this book may be reproduced in any form without written permission from the publisher. Cody Koala™ is a trademark and logo of Pop!.

Printed in the United States of America, North Mankato, Minnesota.

102022
012023

THIS BOOK CONTAINS RECYCLED MATERIALS

Cover Photo: Shutterstock Images
Interior Photos: Shutterstock Images
Editor: Grace Hansen
Series Designer: Colleen McLaren

Library of Congress Control Number: 2022941114

Publisher's Cataloging-in-Publication Data
Names: Andrews, Elizabeth, author.
Title: Scottish fold cats / by Elizabeth Andrews
Description: Minneapolis, Minnesota : Pop!, 2023 | Series: Cats | Includes online resources and index.
Identifiers: ISBN 9781098243142 (lib. bdg.) | ISBN 9781098243845 (ebook)
Subjects: LCSH: Scottish fold cat--Juvenile literature. | Cat, Domestic--Juvenile literature. | Shorthair cat--Juvenile literature. | Zoology--Juvenile literature.
Classification: DDC 636.8--dc23

Table of Contents

Scottish Susie

The Scottish fold is a newer **breed**. The first of its kind was found by a farmer in Scotland in 1961. The cat had **unique** folded ears. The farmer named the cat Susie.

Watch a video here!

Every Scottish fold cat is related to Susie.

single fold

double fold

triple fold

Scottish fold cats are special. They are best known for their folded ears. Ears can have a single fold, double fold, or triple fold. The cats also have round eyes and faces.

Scottish fold cats were originally called "lops."

Scottish fold cats can have a long or short coat. Longhaired Scottish folds have thick, soft fur on their back legs, toes, ears, and tail. Both coat types come in nearly all colors and patterns.

Chapter 2

Personality

Scottish folds are quiet cats. They are laid back and loving toward their owners. The cats often choose a favorite family member to follow around.

Learn more here!

Scottish folds get
along with most people
and animals. They even
enjoy children and dogs!

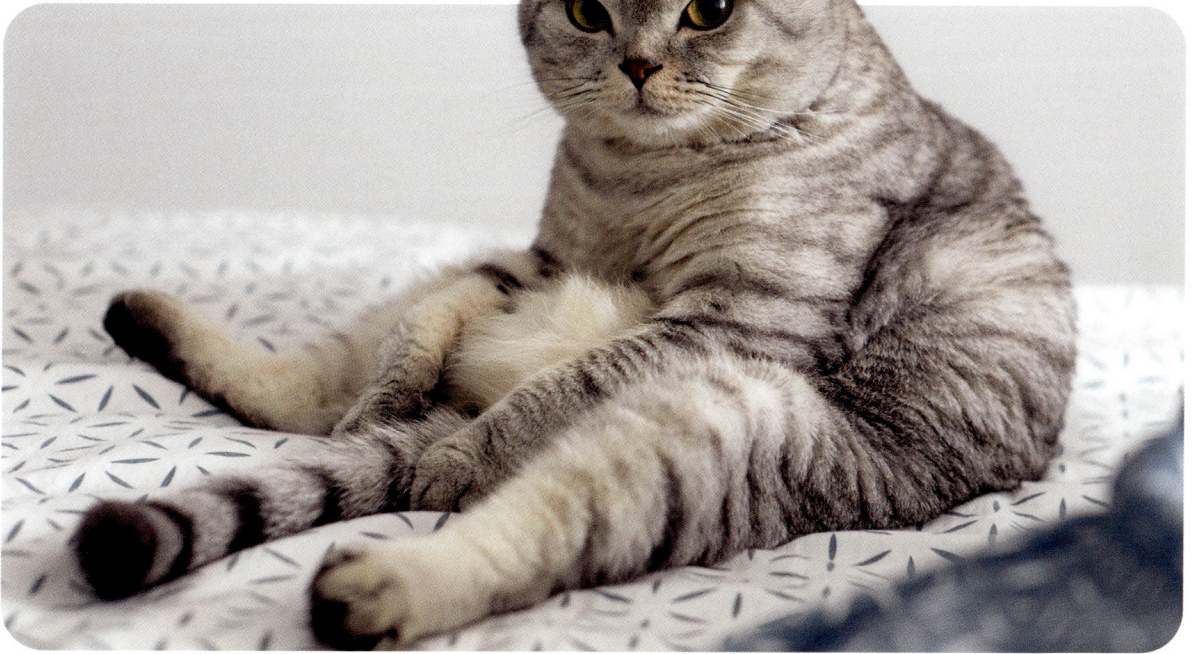

They listen well and like to play. The cats are known for sitting in funny positions.

Scottish folds won't choose to snuggle very often, but they like to be around the people they love.

Chapter 3

Cat Care

Scottish folds like having their fur brushed. Longhaired Scottish folds need to be brushed more often. It's also important to clean their ears. They use **litter boxes** that should be cleaned daily.

Explore links here!

Scottish folds can get sicknesses. They can also have **mobility** problems that may lead to pain. It is important to have a good vet to visit.

Chapter 4

Kittens

Scottish folds are born blind and deaf. They will see and hear around three weeks old. Kittens need to stay with their mother until they are 12 to 16 weeks old.

Complete an activity here!

Not all kittens in a Scottish fold **litter** will get folded ears. It all depends on which **genes** they get from their parents. If a kitten has the gene, its ears will begin to fold at around 21 days old.

Making Connections

Text-to-Self

If you were to get a Scottish fold cat, what kind of ears would you want it to have?

Text-to-Text

Have you read any other books about a breed of cat? If so, how was it similar to and different from the Scottish fold?

Text-to-World

Scottish fold cats are originally from Scotland. Are there any other animals named after the country they come from?

Glossary

breed – a particular type or kind of animal.

gene – information in DNA that affects how animals look and behave.

litter – all kittens born at one time to a mother cat.

litter box – a box filled with cat litter, which is like sand. Cats use litter boxes to bury their waste.

mobility – the quality of moving or being moved easily.

unique – being the only one of its kind.

Index

Online Resources

popbooksonline.com

Thanks for reading this Cody Koala book!

This book is filled with videos, puzzles, games, and more! Scan the QR codes* while you read, or visit the website below to make this book pop.

popbooksonline.com/scottish-fold

*Scanning QR codes requires a web-enabled smart device with a QR code reader app and a camera.